FLAVOR

Faith Love And Victory Over Racism

by

Shirley and John Billy

authorHOUSE®

AuthorHouse™
1663 Liberty Drive
Bloomington, IN 47403
www.authorhouse.com
Phone: 833-262-8899

Published by AuthorHouse 07/31/2020

ISBN: 978-1-4259-8996-5 (sc)
ISBN: 978-1-4520-4099-8 (e)

Foreword

Throughout the ages, men and women have penned memorable stories of love. Almost always, these stories are based on actual events, and even more consistently, the path to bliss is marked by blinding curves and painful thorns.

FLAVOR is no different. This account of "star-crossed lovers" who met in Baltimore, Maryland in 1954 is similar to many other love stories written throughout time all across America. What makes this book unique, however, are the characters themselves and the primary events leading up to their nearly half century of marital happiness.

The fact that John Billy is insistent that this 50-year-old story be told is testimony to his timeless message for young couples today – true love knows no boundaries, be it race, time, or injustice. He and his devoted wife, Shirley, have established new heights for the definition of the phrase "love overcomes all obstacles" and this book describes their journey of realizing this truth.

Doris L. Williams

Acknowledgement

We want to thank our friend and co-writer, Doris
L Williams, for her encouragement and help.
She did extensive and exhaustive research on
our behalf and spent many, many hours on the
computer putting this story all together for us.

We are proud of the fact that Doris, an African
American, was the first female to hold the
position of high school principal in Harford
County, Maryland. She was named to the Harford
County Educators' Hall of Fame in May of 2004.

To us she is a godsend and we deeply
appreciate all her efforts and love.

JOHN & SHIRLEY BILLY

$\mathcal{L}ove$

I Corinthians 13 (*The Good News Bible*, New York: American Bible Society, 1976.)

1. I may be able to speak the languages of men and even of angels, but if I have no love, my speech is no more than a noisy gong or a clanging bell.
2. I may have the gift of inspired preaching; I may have all knowledge and understand all secrets; I may have all the faith needed to move mountains – but if I have no love, I am nothing.
3. I may give away everything I have, and even give up my body to be burned – but if I have no love, this does me no good.
4. Love is patient and kind, it is not jealous or conceited or proud;
5. Love is not ill-mannered or selfish or irritable; love does not keep a record of wrongs;
6. Love is not happy with evil, but is happy with the truth.

7. Love never gives up; and its faith, hope and patience never fail.
8. Love is eternal. There are inspired messages, but they are temporary; there are gifts of speaking in strange tongues, but they will cease; there is knowledge, but it will pass.
9. For our gifts of knowledge and of inspired messages are only partial;
10. But when what is perfect comes, then what is partial will disappear.
11. When I was a child, my speech, feelings, and thinking were all those of a child; now that I am a man, I have no more use for childish ways.
12. What we see now is like a dim image in a mirror, then we shall see face-to-face. What I know now is only partial; then it will be complete – as complete as God's knowledge of me.
13. Meanwhile these three remain: faith, hope, and love; and the greatest of these is love.

Preface
Shirley

My name is Shirley Ann Howard Billy. I was born in Blytheville, Arkansas on June 13, 1936. My mother was Irish and my father, who was from Arkansas, was part Irish and part English. We moved to Baltimore, Maryland, my mother's home, when I was four years old. I grew up on the Eastside in a typically blue-collar neighborhood and graduated from Patterson Park High School in 1955.

This true story is about how genuine love between a man and a woman, specifically my husband and me, overcame and changed a 241-year-old law in the State of Maryland in the mid 1950's. The law stated: "It is illegal for a white woman to bear a child fathered by a Negro."

Contrary to what many may believe, I can truly say that what appealed to me most about John Billy when I first met him, had nothing to do with the color of his skin. It was the person he was on the inside. My family did not display love very openly, especially my mother. Although I'm sure she must have loved me, she never really showed me with a hug or a kiss that I can remember.

John, however, from the moment I first danced with him, was gentle, tender, and so very caring. While I could not fathom what would happen in our futures, I, Shirley Ann Howard, somehow knew this mild, quiet, good-looking, young man was the person who would show me what love was.

Although we endured harassment, hatred, rejection, and all of the customary prejudices that go along with being an interracial couple, we stayed together and as a result of our experiences, today we know the meaning of true and lasting love.

John

My name is John Moses Billy. I am an African-American, born in Washington, DC, on July 27, 1935. When I was five years old, my family moved to Baltimore, Maryland. My mother, Bessie Billy was born in North Carolina and my father, Nathaniel Billy, was born in South Carolina. I was my parent's second born child. My mother died when I was nine years old and, although my father was with the family, mostly my mom's sister, Ethel Pinkney helped my father raise my siblings. I graduated from Baltimore's Carver Vocational High School in 1953. I also attended Larry London Music School on a three-year scholarship where I studied piano. After graduation from high school, I became a recording artist with the "Honey Boys," a Baltimore, doo-wop singing group popular in the mid 1950's. Later, after the "Honey Boys disbanded, I formed my own band – John Billy and the Generators.

617 Bradford, a small street on the Eastside, was the home my parents moved to upon coming to Baltimore and it was the house in which my three brothers, Nathaniel Jr., Ronald, Bobby, two sisters, Mattie and Barbara, and I grew up. I was the second born to two loving and caring parents, who only wanted what was best for their four children. Our house was about 30 feet from a school that we could not attend because it was for white children.

I married my first wife, Myrtle, at the age of seventeen. We lived in that same house on Bradford Street with our two children – Julius and Veronica. Needless to say, because of our ages, the marriage did not last long at all. When Myrtle left and went to live with her sister, for better or for worse, the marriage was over. Later, I came to recognize that this was for better, because I met Shirley and not long after, I left my childhood home for good.

The story being told in this book proves that love and justice can and will overcome racism.

John Billy and the Generators

Chapter One:
The Meeting
John's Memories

The teenage boy walked over to me.

"A young lady on the other side gave me this note to give you. She wants to dance with you."

"Which young lady?"

"She's on the other side of the hall in the corner. She has blonde hair and is wearing a black dress."

Somewhat reluctantly, I walked over to where he had pointed. My dilemma: there were two blonds dressed in black. One was beautiful and the other was really good looking. I asked the prettiest one to dance and she accepted. Every eye in the place was on me. The other members of the Honey Boys got extremely nervous.

I know I will never forget how the first day of the rest of my life started. It was a warm, beautiful Sunday afternoon, in September 1954, one week after Labor Day. Baltimore always had the "I Am An American Day Parade" on this Sunday, organized by *The News American,* one of the popular, local newspapers. This was a parade that everyone came to see. People came from all the surrounding counties and even from other states. Every popular drum core participated. I remember participating with the St. Francis Drum Core when I was only 12 years old. Always interested in music, I played bugle and the drums then.

On this particular day, three of my buddies and I were in our usual places, singing "doo-wop" on the corner. We had a group called the Honey Boys and everyone loved to listen to our unique sound. Of all the groups, and there were many at that time in that section of town, we were the most talked about "doo-woppers" in East Baltimore.

The crowd was cheering us on, when a Jewish fellow came over to me and commented about how good we sounded. He asked if there were any possible way we could perform that night at a private, neighborhood social club. The guys and I agreed to be there at 8:00 pm; only one hour from the time he asked us.

We were there on time. In 1954, whites and blacks did not mix in Baltimore. This social club was for teenagers. Young whites from that entire neighborhood came there to dance the jitterbug and to listen to the rock and roll songs emanating from the mostly white artists that dominated the jukebox. After we finished our three songs, everyone gathered around us, asking for autographs, and congratulating us on how good we sounded.

That's when the young man came up to me with the note and I went looking for the note writer. Dancing with a white girl was totally new to me.

"So what's your name?" I inquired as our bodies swayed to the rhythm of the music.

"Shirley Howard," she responded sweetly. "And yours?"

"My name is Billy! John Billy!"

"Gee, that's different! Seems to me that Billy should be your first name and your last name should be John."

"Well, it's not as if I had any choice. I had to accept what I was given. Where do you live?"

"I live about three blocks from here on Collington Avenue."

"That's only three blocks from my house." I live over on Bradford St.

We hit it off instantly. She appeared to be really interested in who I was and I was very interested in finding out more about her.

When the dance ended, I asked, "This was great! Can I walk you home?"

"Yes!"

"Do you think I can see you again?"

"I don't see why not!"

"I was really surprised when I got your note."

"Oh I didn't send you that note. My best friend, Tea, sent it!"

It was then that I realized I had asked the wrong girl to dance. Shirley was not the writer of the note.

"Oh - Oh! Do you think I should go over and dance with her?"

"I don't think that's a good idea now! Do you?"

"Maybe I can take you out tomorrow night, and then maybe take Tea out the next night," I suggested jokingly.

It was very obvious that she was not going for that idea. When I walked her home that night from the club, I told her I'd call. Later in the week, we made arrangements to meet on the corner not far from the social club. Reluctant about coming alone, Shirley asked if I could arrange for one of the other guys in the group to take out Tea.

"No problem!" I said.

Shirley's Memories

It was a warm, sunny day in September 1954. My best friend, Tea, and I were on our way to the last rite of summer – the "I Am An American Day Parade" at Patterson Park. This was a huge parade that everyone in Baltimore attended every year. School would be opening in two weeks and we were so excited. This was our senior year; then we'd be on our own. Life was good!

There were so many things going on that day. We even stopped to listen to four young Negro men singing doowop on the corner. They were very good and a crowd had gathered around to listen.

After the parade ended, Tea and I went back to her grandmother's house. There was a teen center around the corner. The club itself wasn't much, but there were lots of teens who gathered there, and that night, the "Honey Boys" would be singing there. The neighborhood teens were all crazy about them, but I had never heard of them.

I was really surprised when I got there and saw that the "Honey Boys" were the same group that had been singing on the corner earlier that day at the parade. Everyone enjoyed their singing, including me, especially since I had never seen a real, live, singing group.

When they finished their performance, "Goodnight Sweetheart" was playing on the jukebox.

"I want to dance with one of the singers," Tea whispered to me.

"Go ahead!" I said.

Tea wrote a note and handed it to one of the teenage white guys and told him specifically which singer to give it. A minute later, the singer came over and asked me to dance and pulled me out on the floor.

"I think you've got the wrong girl! My friend Tea ..."

"I'll dance with her later!" he interrupted.

I felt so excited dancing with him. During the dance, I learned that John Billy was his name. He was good looking and I liked him right away. I had never before given any thought to dating Negro men, but after the dance, I gave him my phone number. He was so attentive and I liked him immediately.

The club closed at 10:00 pm. I started home and John, who lived only three blocks from my house, began walking with me. It had gotten chilly and there weren't many people on the street or sitting on their steps hanging around outside. We got a block away from my house and said goodnight. Although neither of us spoke it, we knew it was not safe for John to walk me all the way to my door. He told me he would call me.

The next day my mother got about five phone calls from neighbors telling her I was walking down the street with a Negro boy. When she asked me about it, I told her the truth.

"We met at the club and he happened to be walking home in the same direction and didn't think it was safe for me to walk by myself. I didn't do anything wrong, did I?"

"No!" Mom said. "Just don't do it again and stay away from that club! You hear me!"

I agreed and I kept my promise. I never went back to the club and I never walked down that street with John again. But I never stopped thinking about him after that first night. It was exciting, just to daydream about doing something so forbidden. Little did I know what I was setting myself up for. I couldn't wait for him to call me. He didn't have a phone at home, so I couldn't call him. Nor would I!

Finally, John did call. The first conversation lasted about two hours. He was very easy to talk with and I so enjoyed talking with him. I went to bed that night elated. We had made a date to meet in a couple of days.

Chapter Two:
The First Date

The day that we set to meet finally arrived and the two girls met the other member of the group and me on the corner. I spent a long time prepping him for the date, reviewing what he should do and what he should not do. Since I lived alone in the Bradford Street house, we decided to go and hang out at my place.

I couldn't wait to be with Shirley again. The few moments we had already shared together were, complete joy and utter pleasure for me. I was in a world I had never been before; a world I never knew existed. I never realized that anyone could create a world like this for me and I wanted her for the rest of my life. That quickly, I was truly in love – heart and soul!

Although I wanted her forever, a sense of reality engulfed my thinking. It was taboo for a black man to be with a white woman. Further, what I had not revealed to Shirley was that I, John Billy, am a married man. My wife left me two months ago and went to stay with her sister. Somehow, I had to tell Shirley about this – but later, not now.

The music was playing softly and that first kiss was so exciting. I had stayed up at night dreaming about our first time being together and waiting for this moment. I was in a dream world that was hard for me to believe had come true.

At that very moment, there was a hard knock at the door. I was awakened from my dream of pleasure and fell into a nightmare. My first thought was that it must be the police. Someone must have seen two white girls coming into my house and called the police. I peeped through the blinds. To my surprise, it was my estranged wife. Until I heard her voice, I never expected a visit from her. I didn't have the heart to tell Shirley about my marital situation that night. I wanted to explain it in private. I told her it was my sister.

Embarrassed, I asked my buddy to take the girls out the back door and make sure they got home safely. He quickly escorted the two girls out. Myrtle, my estranged wife, had stopped by that night just to find out who I was seeing. She thought maybe she could even see for herself. Luckily, she missed the girls.

The next day, I called Shirley hoping to explain my marital situation.

"Hi Shirl, I hope you're okay. Listen I called to explain about last night…"

"John, I'm sorry but I can't talk right now, My mother got a call this morning from one of the neighbors in the next block. They told her they saw Tea and me walking home with a Negro last night, and she is really mad. I told her it wasn't you and that made her madder, She thinks I'm lying and now I'm being punished. I have to stay in the house indefinitely and I'm not allowed to use the phone. I've got to get off the phone before she comes in from out back and catches me. Talk to you later! Bye!"

I was devastated as she quickly got off the phone.

Two weeks passed. I tried to call but her mother always answered the phone so I had to hang up. One day when I called, by luck, Shirley answered. Her mother wasn't home. We both admitted that we had missed each other greatly. She agreed to see me again. While I knew that I was already in love, this confirmed that her feelings for me were growing.

Chapter Three:
Hate!

Shirley was 18 and about to graduate from Patterson Park High School the day her mother found out John was married. This is her story.

After I had been seeing John for some time, I was upstairs in my bedroom when my mother called me to come down. When I got downstairs, there were two Negro women standing in our living room. One of them had told my mother that I was going with her husband. I truly thought she was someone trying to start trouble for me – maybe one of John's old girlfriends.

"I am not seeing anyone's husband. I don't even know who you are!"

She reached into her pocket and pulled out a picture of me. It was the graduation picture I had given John. I was surprised but still didn't think he was married, because he was so young. I had been to his house quite a few times and there was never any evidence of a wife.

My mother wrote down her address and told her it was time for her (my mother) to meet John Billy. I did not go to John's house with my mother. She took her girlfriend with her. She never talked to me about her visit and I never inquired about what transpired, or even if she talked with him.

By this time, although I was beginning to have doubts about a lot of things John had told me, I knew I did not want our relationship to end. While I was heartbroken by this turn of events, I guess I just didn't want him to be married. The whole thing was becoming a real nightmare. At that moment, I felt, that nothing would ever be the same again.

A part of me wanted him and his wife to work things out. I did not want to be involved with a married man. However, a larger part of me still ached for him. I had never felt like this before. I was also extremely angry with him for not telling me. If I had known from the beginning, there would have been no relationship at all. The problem now was it was too late. I wanted him; I was in love with him. There was nothing anyone could say or do that could possibly change that.

Shirley's mother became more intent than ever on keeping us apart. The only way I could talk with her was to have a young girl call and ask for her and then I got on the phone. This was our only form of communication for several weeks but I still couldn't tell her about my marital situation over the phone.

Eventually, we met secretly and face-to-face, apologetically, I explained my marital status. I got married at the age of 17, because my girlfriend was pregnant. It lasted less than two years. Now at the age of 20, I was separated from my wife and two children, trying to file for a divorce. The marriage was a mistake and we were much too young to have said, "I do."

The Honey Boys were playing in a club not too far from where she lived. One day, Shirley told me her mother had found out I sung with the group and since where we were performing was widely publicized throughout the neighborhood; her mother was coming to the club to shoot me! I was really nervous. Shirley's mother was coming to shoot me!

The club at which we were performing was segregated. While Blacks could work and entertain there; they could not sit, eat, or socialize with the customers. If not performing, the "Honey Boys" had to stand in the corner and talk or go outside and stand. That night, while taking a break outside, Shirley's stepfather approached me, told me who he was and said he wanted to talk with me. He said her mother sent him to talk about my not seeing Shirley anymore. He indicated it really didn't mean anything to him, but he was doing what her mother wanted him to do. Just to satisfy the issue, I agreed not to see Shirley again. I knew I was lying when

I said it. He went back and told her mother about our agreement.

I called Shirley the next day. In fact, I called her three to five times a week, but I could not see her or spend time with her. We were missing each other more and more. Thinking about our first time together made it hard to be apart. I knew I couldn't live without her. I needed her and felt she needed me.

Chapter Four:
Too Many Risks

A month went by! We'd talk on the phone but we still couldn't see each other. After Shirley graduated from high school, her mother started giving her a little more freedom. We started seeing each other again, more often than before. This was more exciting than the first time we went out.

I had to be at work by 7:00 in the morning. Shirley would get up at 3:00 am and meet me at an all night restaurant about four blocks from where she lived. We talked, drank coffee, and just looked into each other's eyes until time for me to go to work. Sometimes, we would run into each other "accidentally on purpose" at the grocery store or anywhere else we could talk. Although we were seeing each other and being together three or four times a week, Shirley simply refused to return to my house where I lived as a married man. Most of the time, she agreed to be with me at the houses of my friends, or in the car.

One night we were parked on a lot. Someone knocked on the window while we were making love. I couldn't see whom it was because the windows were all fogged up from our passion. I quickly pulled up my pants and went outside.

There were two guys standing there and I knew what they wanted. I told them this was my main lady and there was no way they were getting what I knew they wanted. They knew I was serious and would fight. They stared at me; I glared back at them and they finally realized I would die before I let them do to Shirley what I knew they wanted to do. They left.

I know that it was God in control of this situation, and I was eternally grateful to Him. I stood there motionless for a few minutes and began to think about what could have happened. There were two guys and I was only one. These two knew me as a member of the "Honey Boys" and probably respected that. They also knew I was a boxer because I was known in the neighborhood for winning boxing tournaments, but they could have had a weapon. I had nothing. There was absolutely nothing I could have done.

I could not tell Shirley what really happened. I had to lie to her because I did not want to frighten her. I simply told her it was something the guys wanted to ask me about; someone's address they thought I could give them.

However, I knew then that we could not continue meeting like we were doing. I had to do something. After all, because she was white and I was black, I knew we were already walking on really thin ice. It was up to me to make it safe for both of us.

On the streets of Baltimore were white men who wouldn't accept a white woman with a black man. Likewise, we had to contend with the black females who did not like me being with a white woman. The real danger, however, lied with the police who would see a black and white couple in the car and stop them for no reason. Sometimes, while driving down the streets, obscene names were yelled at us. Whenever we went to or met at someone's house, in order to distract attention from us, I would go in first, by myself. Then Shirley would come in by herself.

I needed a place of my own. I needed a place I had not shared with any other woman and where Shirley would feel free to come.

I got a two-bedroom house on Chapel Street in East Baltimore and Shirley, who had gotten a job after graduation, was comfortable coming to my new place anytime. Usually, she stopped by four or five times a week. It was a blessing not to have to meet in the projects, in alleys, around dark corners, in the woods, or anywhere else along "Ghetto Boulevard." Now I felt like I had gone "up the freeway." I was beginning to feel free and safe.

We slept on an Army cot together and had a milk cart for our night table. It was not much but we were content just to be together in our own place. Shirley would come almost everyday and that made me very happy and pleased.

After a year of our secret rendezvous, Shirley became pregnant. She was still living with her mother but I wanted her to be with me. She wouldn't because I was still married. I called her everyday.

Shirley Ann Howard - July, 1956

Chapter Five:
Shirley's Pregnancy

I was ready to graduate from high school. My senior year I started working for Esskay under the school's Work Study Program. After I graduated they asked me to stay. I loved this job. John and I were seeing each other on a regular basis. Then I became pregnant. Luckily, I did not show until the very end. I don't think I ever saw my mother madder than she was on the day I told her I was pregnant. In fact, this was one of the hardest things I ever had to do in my nineteen years of life. After all of the yelling, screaming, and quarreling were over, she said to me in the cruelest tone possible, "you are not allowed to bring that baby into my house!" I had to quit my job. In those days, it was disgraceful to be with child and not married, let alone give birth to the child of a black man.

June 7, 1956, I gave birth to a baby boy at Johns Hopkins Hospital. John was not allowed to see our baby. The entire hospital was in an uproar when they found out the baby had been fathered by a Negro and had been given birth by a white mother. The story of my treatment in that hospital is unbelievable.

If you ask any woman to list the happiest days of her life, most would say, "one is the day my child was born," and rightly so. That's exactly the way I felt when I realized my baby was coming. I was so excited and looking forward to seeing my baby, but things started going terribly wrong.

The day I went to the hospital in labor, my mother went with me. Evidently, she talked to someone while I was in labor. She told them my story and said that I could not bring the child home to her house. By the time I was ready to deliver, it seemed everyone was aware that my child was bi-racial. After my son was born, I was taken to the Negro Ward. The nurse there told my nurse to "take me down to the white area" as I had no business being there in the Negro Ward. When we got back to the White Ward, the nurse was told to take me back to the Negro Ward. No one wanted me.

There was nothing but confusion and ugly discussions about what to do with me. This made me mad, sad, and frightened. I stayed in the Negro Ward one day and the next day was taken to a private room. People kept coming and going; asking me questions. I was in the hospital for nine days because my temperature would not go down.

My visitors were not the typical visitors that most new mothers get. I was not allowed to see my baby's father. Neither friends nor family members came to visit. My visitors came from social services, child welfare, St. Elizabeth's Orphanage. St. Elizabeth's personnel told me they would take care of my baby until something was settled. If I wanted him living with me, first I had to get my own place to live, get a job, and prove I was capable of taking care of him myself. I was sick because I didn't know how long it would take me to do these things.

I went home to my mother's house feeling depressed, lonely, and heartsick. I had given birth to a beautiful baby boy but did not have him with me and did not know if I ever would get him.

I got a job at the telephone company. I was thrilled to have it. I passed all the tests and they seemed happy with me. I had the job about two weeks and then it happened. Early one Friday morning at about 3:00 am, I was awakened by a hard knock at the front door of my mother's house. When I opened it, the police served me with an indictment from the Grand Jury, and charged me with fornication. The Grand Jury indicted me for violating Section 513 of Article 27 of the Public General Laws of Maryland.

The police did not park in front of the house, so I was walked around the corner and placed in the paddy wagon. I was taken to the Pine Street Jail for Women, where I spent the night by myself in a dismal, dirty cell crying continuously. I was 20 years old and incarcerated.

I just couldn't believe what was happening to me. Within a few weeks, I had given birth to my baby, came home from the hospital without him, and then was arrested.

The day after I was incarcerated, my mother came and picked me up. She put her house up as collateral to cover the $1,000 bond. She had made arrangements for a lawyer and I met with him that same day I got out, She was adamant that her lawyer would work toward keeping a lot of the events private and out of the newspapers. However, how well I remember the headlines, "Love Baby Hassle," in the *Afro-American Newspaper* that focused on my son. White people were standing across the street from my mother's house just looking to see the "harlot blond" who had given birth to a Negro's baby.

My mother was getting a lot of bad phone calls. For my safety and hers, she asked me to go live with my aunt. My aunt agreed.

I only missed one day of work - the Friday I was arrested. I called in and told them I had an accident but that I would be in on Monday.

When I went back to work, I thought everything was okay. I worked another week before I got called into the office. They asked me if I was the same Shirley Howard who was arrested for giving birth to a baby fathered by a Negro. I said "yes" and with that response, I was fired.

A couple of weeks later I got a job as a clerk at Marlboro Shirt Company. I worked there for about four weeks before being fired for the same reason. I was crushed. I needed a job to get my son back.

My cousin's girlfriend was working for Key Wine and Liquor. She said they had an opening. I went there and got the job. She also was living with an older lady who was having money problems. She was renting a room from her. I decided to move out of my aunt's house and also rent a room from Mary. It was a very nice house and we had full use of it. Mary knew all about me and didn't care. She was very nice, kind, and considerate.

I liked living at Mary's because I could come and go as I pleased. This meant I could see John whenever I wanted to see him. It was an ideal situation. John worked weekends until 2:00 am. I would leave my house and meet him at his. I was happy; he was happy. The only thing missing was our son, but things were definitely coming together. I had a good job, a place to live, and John was waiting for his divorce. Plus, he had his place and I was planning to move into it, but I would not do that until his divorce became final.

Mom's lawyer was successful in keeping much of the court proceedings private. He told me not to come to the trial so I never attended. After the grand jury indictment, very little appeared in the local newspapers about the case.

When the time came for Shirley to be released from the hospital, her mother would not allow her to bring the baby home. She wanted her to put him up for adoption. The hospital placed him in St. Elizabeth's, an orphanage. Shirley left the hospital and went back to her mother's house.

I was emotionally distraught. I couldn't talk to the woman I loved more than life. I'd called her house. Her mother answered. I hung up! I had never seen and was not allowed to see the precious child that was a result of our love for each other.

One night the incredible happened. At 3:00 am, the police came and arrested Shirley. They took her to the Pine Street Jail for Women. I found out about Shirley's arrest when I read it in the *Baltimore Morning Sun*. Shirley Howard was arrested on a statue written on the Maryland law books in 1715, over 241 years ago. The statute declared that it was against the law for a white woman to bear a child fathered by a Negro. Shirley's arrest was the first time the law had ever been enforced.

Later that day, the police came and took me to court. I had to stand before the judge and testify that I was the father of Shirley's child. When I got home that evening, there were business cards from five lawyers, wanting to take the case free of charge. They all wanted to defend us.

Shirley stayed in jail overnight. The lawyer got her released from jail on a $1,000 bond. Her mother insisted that no other lawyer but hers would defend the case.

I was still not allowed to talk to Shirley. The only way I learned any details regarding her case was through the newspapers. *The Baltimore Sunpapers, News American, and* the *Afro American* all ran the story. Everywhere I went, I was asked about the case. It was the talk of Baltimore in August of 1956. Both the Maryland Civil Liberties Union and the NAACP sought permission to sit in on the case as "friends of the court." In April 1957, a judge ruled the statute discriminating and declared that it violated the 14th Amendment to the Constitution.

I was afraid that someone would hurt Shirley. Her mother asked her to promise that she would stay away from me for good, but there was no way that either of us could keep the promises we had made because we were deeply in love, more committed than ever to being with each other, and intent on eventually getting our baby back.

I started working on getting my divorce, finding a better job, and insuring that I have a better place in which all of us could live,

I wanted so much to see our baby, I went to St. Elizabeth's but they would not allow me to see him. His name was listed as John Howard. The caseworker said the only way I could see him was if I were with his mother.

I called Shirley and we made arrangements for both of us to go together to see our son. We met on a parking lot. After almost two months from the day he was born, I finally saw our handsome son. He was the most beautiful baby I had ever seen. At that moment, I made a silent promise to Johnny that it would not be long before Billy would be added as his last name.

After that visit, I knew I had to hurry and get my family together. I got a better job. My divorce was pending.

I knew we would have to get married before we could have our baby back. We visited Johnny two and three times a week. Each time we left him, our hurt was greater. After one of our visits, we thought about kidnapping him,

We wanted our baby so badly and couldn't imagine anyone keeping our child from us. When we visited him at St. Elizabeth, we could take him out into the garden playground for children. Most of the time, we were by ourselves, just the three of us. What would happen if we just walked away with our child? After all he was ours. Is it really kidnapping if you take your own child? Then we took the time to think about our plight. Shirley was out on bail! My divorce was pending! The law was against us!

We decided against doing it. We realized we would never be together if we did that. We kissed Johnny and took him back into the orphanage, but even more determined that we would get our son back soon.

January 20, 1957
Shirley Howard and son, Johnny (Age 7 months old)
Visiting at St. Elizabeth's Orphanage

January 20, 1957
John Billy and son, Johnny (Age 7 months old)
Visiting at St. Elizabeth's Orphanage

Chapter Six:
Prejudice Comes In All Colors

Finally Shirley decided she had to get away from her mother's house. She moved in with her girlfriend. As much as we wanted it, we both knew she could not live with me, because we didn't want anything to interfere with getting Johnny back. Also, Shirley had not yet gone to trial and we had to insure that nothing would be done to prevent her from being found innocent.

One day, Shirley and her girlfriend, came over to my house. One of my buddies had also stopped by. We were all just relaxing and talking. All of a sudden, with no warning, my front door was completely torn from the hinges. A policeman was standing over us.

"I want you two women to get out – NOW!" He said.

"What's the problem Officer? I asked.

"I said I want them out! I don't want any of this kind of carrying on going on on by beat! Get out, NOW!"

Shirley and her friend left immediately. We all had to yield to his demands. There was nothing we could do.

Later, I learned that it was my Negro neighbors who called the police and complained that white women were meeting Negro men in my house. One woman in particular indicated that they (the neighbors) did not want any white women coming into my house or any house on the block, especially to see a Negro man. Even though it was my house, there was nothing I could do. I wanted no problems. Shirley was fighting for her freedom and I was fighting for her and my son.

I realized from all that we had been through up to this point, that it is not easy living in a city where it seems like everything is against you – people you don't know, people you know very well, and especially "the system." When you feel like this, and the load really seems hard to bear, that's when you have to be really strong.

Chapter Seven:
Uncle Sam Gets Involved

Everyday, someone asked me what was going to happen, and everyone was expecting the worst, All I could do was trust in God and think positively!

Finally, I got a job driving a truck for a furniture store, making a little more money than I had ever gotten in the past. I was satisfied and excited about this new job. Surely now, I would be able to bring my family together.

After being at the furniture store for three months, I came home from work and in my mailbox was a letter – Greetings from Uncle Sam! I almost fell out. I just couldn't believe it. For one reason, I was still married to my first wife. At that time they were not drafting men with two young children and now I had three. In addition, there was no war going on; America was at peace when this father of three children was drafted. When I got that letter, I was sure I had been "blackballed" and had been sent a "special" invitation to join the Army. They would do anything to separate Shirley and me. Still, I had no choice; I had to go.

The next day I went to work and told my boss. In three weeks I would have to leave my job and report to the Army. At the end of the first week before I was to leave, I was called into the office and told I was fired. The reason – if you're working at a job and you are drafted, the job is required to hold your position for you until you get out. They did not want to hold my position open, so they fired me that first week after I got the notice.

I wanted Shirley to continue maintaining the house until I got back. The day I left was probably the most depressing day of my life. I had to leave the place I had known as home most of my life, and even worse, I had to leave the one woman whom I dearly loved more than life. I just couldn't bear the thought of being away from Shirley for any length of time, especially when we were separated from our baby.

I was sent to Fort Jackson, South Carolina. This was the first time I had ever been south. It was also the first time I had not been in the same city as Shirley since we met. It hurt me tremendously to be away from her and our baby.

I met a captain in the Army who was from Baltimore. He knew who I was and about my situation because of what he had read in the newspaper. He had read about our case and immediately confided that he felt this was not the time for me to be in the Army. He offered a proposal of how I could get out after I finished basic training.

While the bad news was I was in the Army hundreds of miles away from Shirley, one day I received some good news. Shirley sent me a letter telling me that my divorce was, at last, final. That letter erased all of the sadness and loneliness that I had been feeling since coming to Ft. Jackson. I got back my old unwavering, John Billy personality. I had one week to go before basic training was over and then I was going home for two weeks. Marriage was the only thing I had on my mind. I knew from Shirley's letters that she felt the same way.

As soon as I completed basic training, I went home to Baltimore and we were together again. This was a completely thrilling and fulfilling time in my life. That first night home it seemed as if we were trying to make up for all the lost time we were away from each other. It was like the first time we met – all over again.

On June 21, 1958, Shirley Ann Howard married John M. Billy. Since mixed race marriages were not allowed to be conducted in Baltimore, we went to Washington, DC, the place where I was born.

My father, Nathaniel Billy, took us to get our marriage license and we were married at my Aunt Mary Gibson's house on Longfellow Street. Only a handful of my relatives, and none of Shirley's, were there, but it didn't matter. We were young, in love and so happy on that day. After we married, I knew I had to hurry and get out of the Army so that we could get our baby and live a wonderful life together.

John Moses Billy - 1958

When I returned to Ft. Jackson, I started the process of getting the Army to give me a hardship discharge. I did exactly what the Captain told me to do and was pleased when it did not take very long. After a month I received an honorable discharge and went back to Baltimore.

Shirley and I were together again, this time as man and wife. All we needed was our baby to make us complete. Unfortunately, this wasn't easy.

Soon after I returned from the Army, Shirley was fired from her job. She had been working at the telephone company. Later she was fired from two other jobs – always for the same reason, her arrest for having a baby fathered by a Negro, that 241-year-old Maryland law. Meanwhile, we called social workers and filled out mountains of paper in order to find out where our son was. He was no longer at the St. Elizabeth's Orphanage.

Still we were not discouraged. We were determined to find our baby and bring him home to live with us. We were broken hearted when we eventually found out that Johnny was being prepared for adoption. He had been living with a family in South Carolina who had entered the final phases of making his adoption permanent. By this time, Johnny was walking. In order for us to stop the adoption, Shirley and I had to prove we were his natural parents and that we were living together as man and wife. Within a week, he was back at the orphanage.

The day we got Johnny out of St. Elizabeth's Orphanage was an extraordinary day in our marriage and in our lives. Finally, we had our baby and he was where he was suppose to be – with us. I had kept my promise to Johnny. At that point in time, I knew I would be with Shirley for the rest of my life. I knew that I loved and was devoted to her. There was nothing she had to prove to me. She had shown me her love and I knew it was from the bottom of her heart. Now, we were inseparable and no one could keep our family apart.

Chapter Eight:
Justice Prevails

Perhaps we will never know all that went on legally regarding Shirley's arrest, the ensuing court case, *State of Maryland v. Shirley Ann Howard*, and the eventual ruling by Chief Judge Emory Hamilton Niles declaring the law unconstitutional, but much information can be gathered from the April 24, 1957, issue of *The Daily Record*. Needles to say, as we look back over them, all of the events were, even at that time, strange and questionable to both of us for several reasons.

Shirley was arrested and indicted by the grand jury on a law established in 1715 that carried real prison time. A sentence of eighteen months to five years was especially frightening for a 20-year old woman who had never been arrested.

The 241-year old statute stated:

"Any white woman who shall suffer or permit herself to be got with child by a colored man or mulatto, upon conviction thereof in the court having criminal jurisdiction, either in the city or county where such child was begotten, or where the same was born, shall be sentenced to the Penitentiary for not less than 18 months nor more than five years."

Another unusual aspect was the timing of the events. Johnny was born on June 7, 1956. The grand jury returned an informal charge against Shirley on August 3, 1956. She was arrested a few days after the indictment was issued. The law was declared unconstitutional on April 22, 1957. According to newspaper articles about the case (*Baltimore Afro American, August 4, 1956)* a year earlier a white woman in Havre de Grace, MD, was acquitted on this charge. It was questionable as to how and who alerted the state's attorney's office on the racial aspects of Shirley's case and this particular law. Hers was apparently the only known prosecution of anyone in Maryland under the statute.

WHITE MOM UPSETS 242-YEAR-OLD RACE LAW, SEEKS HER NEGRO BABY

When Baltimore police hustled white, 20-year-old Shirley Ann Howard off to jail last August, it marked the first time that a 242-year-old Maryland miscegenation law had ever been enforced. Charged with the crime of bearing a Negro's child, faced with a possible five-year sentence, the Arkansas-born blonde spent a night in jail while friends scraped together a $1,000 bond.

"Then and there I decided to clear my name," Shirley told JET in an exclusive interview. "The law was silly. White men have been giving babies to colored women for years and nobody has done a thing about it. But they wanted to throw the book at me." Refusing to believe herself a criminal, she hired Atty. John J. O'Connor, who promptly attacked the miscegenation law's constitutionality. Last week, Baltimore's distinguished Judge Emory H. Niles ruled it "discriminatory" and in violation of the 14th Amendment.

Shirley's case had grown out of her love for 21-year-old commercial sign painter John Moses Billy. An avid jazz fan, she had met him about two years ago in a Baltimore night club, where he was appearing with the Honey Boys Quartet. Recalling their frequent dates, Shirley said nostalgically: "He was kind of nice." But Billy's ardor cooled after the baby was born.

Angered, Shirley slapped a bastardy charge on Billy in Baltimore's Domestic Relations Bureau, succeeded in forcing him to pay her hospital expenses and $7-a-week support for the baby. But her victory backfired. The officials decided to prosecute her when they learned her lover was a Negro.

Even though she won again when the law was declared unconstitutional, she was still a criminal to her family and unsympathetic outsiders. Rejected by her parents, she had long since moved in with a girl friend. Fired

Lying in crib at St. Elizabeth's Orphanage in Baltimore, month-old John Howard is reason for court fight.

John Moses Billy is father of baby, but also married man.

Baby's mother, Shirley Ann Howard, hopes to marry Billy.

I Want My Boy To Be 'A Real American' Says Shirley

from her job as a telephone operator, she was working incognito as an office secretary. Meanwhile, hundreds of poison pen letters poured in, and, worst of all, police hounded her. Only recently they trailed her to a Negro neighborhood, then broke down the door of an apartment she entered.

Despite all the abuse, Shirley was hoping last week that she could eventually marry Billy. Confronting her, however, was the stubborn fact that he is already married and the father of two children. Though separated from his wife, Myrtle, for two years, Billy cannot obtain a quick divorce in Maryland.

Meanwhile, Shirley's major concern is 10-month-old John Howard, presently living at St. Elizabeth's Orphanage in Baltimore. Although she has permission to visit her son, orphanage supervisors bar Billy, claiming he must secure approval from city officials.

But in the midst of the controversy Shirley remains optimistic. Said she: "I have my own life to live. Nobody can judge for me. I'm going to rear that boy to become a real American citizen, and the color of his skin won't be a handicap."

Viewing photograph of his son, Billy is barred from visiting him at orphanage.

RELIGION

Ike Urges Action By Interracial Faith Group

President Eisenhower sent his "best wishes" to a conference of southern church leaders studying the religious implications of racial tension, and asked for "new plans and effective programs to make service of God and neighbor meaningful."

White Mass, Church Ordains Negro Pastor

Rev. Joseph R. Washington, a 26-year-old Negro minister with two white congregations, was ordained at Woburn First Baptist Church in Woburn, Mass. He once served as associate minister at the church.

Rev. M. L. King Jr. Declines N. Y. Pastorate

Rev. Martin Luther King Jr., Montgomery bus boycott leader, refused to accept the pastorate of the $350,000 Union Baptist Church in New York last November because he felt he was needed in the South, JET learned. A spokesman for the 58-year-old, 3,500-member church disclosed that a letter had been sent to Rev. King by church trustees, who offered him the pulpit. But Rev. King told JET he feels the South still needs him.

Dinner Talk: Huddling at the annual Men's Club Father and Son Banquet in Chicago's Quinn Chapel AME Church, guest speaker State's Atty. Benjamin S. Adamowski (l.) and banquet co-chairman Lt. John D. Chamberlain (c.) go over program notes with Quinn Chapel pastor, Rev. Archibald J. Carey Jr.

Much of what was reported in the media was very inaccurate and the court proceedings were quite unusual. Other than the one time I had to appear before the grand jury to testify that I was the father of Shirley's child, neither of us participated in any of the court proceedings. Despite what was reported by the *Afro*, *Jet* magazine, and other publications, I never paid child support nor covered the costs of the baby's birth, although if asked, I would have been honored, not obligated, to do so. If I had been allowed to do this, perhaps it would have been easier for me to see my son. Neither Shirley nor I are quite sure how the hospital expenses were paid. Neither of us was ever interviewed by anyone other than our lawyers. This includes the media, despite what the article says.

Shirley's indictment was eventually dismissed by Judge Niles and declared unconstitutional because it discriminated against the 14th Amendment rights of white women. Her lawyer, John J. O'Connor, Jr., and two lawyers for the Maryland Branch of the American Civil Liberties Union, Francis D. Murnaghan, Jr. and Fred E. Weisgal, (amicus curiac) presented historical research that the statute was originally enacted in 1699 and then changed in 1715. The 1699 statute included the provision that white men convicted of getting Negro women pregnant would be subjected to the same penalties as the white woman. When the new law (1715) was enacted, this provision was omitted.

The fact that the law imposed a penalty against one class of people – white women – for a given offense that is different from other groups of people – white or black men and black women – for the same offense is what made the court declare the law unconstitutional and discriminating. The court ruled that the statute "violates the principle of equal protection of the law under the 14th Amendment to the Constitution of the United States." In other words, Shirley was being punished because of her race and sex rather than because of the crime itself. The 241-year old law, unlike the original 1699 law, only pertained to a crime being committed by white women.

After the decision was made, my lawyer, the biggest black law firm in Baltimore at the time, called us into his office and asked us to get married in Baltimore. He wanted to fight the issue of mixed race marriages being prohibited in the State of Maryland, another law that still existed. Shirley refused because she did not want to get arrested again and go through the same thing all over again. To her credit, she had paid her dues and we both agreed that this law needed to be fought by some other couple. That's when we decided to get married in Washington, DC, where we knew our union would be legal.

Criminal·Court of Baltimore

STATE OF MARYLAND
vs.
SHIRLEY ANN HOWARD

J. Harold Grady, State's Attorney and *Joseph G. Koutz,* Assistant State's Attorney, for the State.

John J. O'Connor, Jr., for the defendant.

Francis D. Murnaghan, Jr. and *Fred E. Weisgal,* for the Maryland Branch of the American Civil Liberties Union, *amicus curiae.*

Criminal Law—Motion To Dismiss Indictment—Violation·Of·Section·513 Of Article 27 Of Public General Laws Of Maryland—Validity Of Statute.

NILES, C. J.—

This case comes before the Court on a motion to dismiss an indictment against the defendant for violating Sec. 513 of Article 27 of the Public General Laws of Maryland, which provides as follows:

"Any white woman who shall suffer or permit herself to be got with child by a Negro or mulatto, upon conviction thereof in the Court having criminal jurisdiction, either in the city or county where such child was begotten or where the same was born, shall be sentenced to the penitentiary for not less than eighteen months nor more than five years."

Historical research by counsel for the defendant indicates that this statute was enacted in different form in 1699 (Acts 1699 c. 43) ; the annotations in the Code are to the effect that in its present form it was enacted in 1715 (Acts 1715, c. 44, sec. 25).

It also appears that the original act of 1699 contained a provision that any white man convicted of having gotten any Negro woman with child should undergo the same penalties as a white woman; but this provision was apparently repealed by omission from the Code of 1860, and is not contained in the present Code.

The statute now under consideration was thus enacted more than 250 years ago. No case has been decided by the Court of Appeals of Maryland in which its validity has been passed upon. The Court is informed also that as far as can be ascertained the present case is the only prosecution under this statute ever brought in the City of Baltimore.

The question presented is whether the statute is valid.

Arguments have been earnestly presented by counsel, to the effect that the statute is invalid by reason of its being obsolete; that it is void as being too vague to be enforceable, since the words "white woman," "Negro," and "mulatto" are not defined, and that no standards are therein contained whereby the Court may reach an exact definition; that these words have changed in meaning since 1696 when the statute was first enacted; that the statute invades the defendant's civil rights; and that the statute is void under the principles set forth in the recent school segregation case of Brown vs. Board of Education, (1954) 347 U. S. 483.

In the view taken by the Court, it is unnecessary to express an opinion on these points, since the decision is controlled by the basic principle that a statute is not valid if it prescribes different punishments or penalties for the same type of conduct when engaged in by persons of different race or color.

The statute penalizes conduct resulting in the procreation of children of mixed race. Four separate categories of persons may by their conduct cause a woman to become pregnant by illicit sexual intercourse with a member of another race, namely, a white man, a white woman, a Negro man and a Negro woman. Sexual intercourse between any of these persons, if of different race and sex, may result in the conception of a child of mixed race. A penalty is imposed, however, only upon a white woman who participates in such conduct. No penalty is imposed upon the Negro man involved. Furthermore, if a Negro woman should become pregnant by a white man, no penalty is imposed upon either the man or the woman.

The basic principle invoked by the defendant was stated by the Supreme Court of the United States in Pace vs. Alabama (1882) 106 U. S. 583, cited by both sides herein. In that case a statute of Alabama prescribed a penalty for fornication or adultery, and a more severe penalty for such conduct where the participants were of different races; no distinction was made as to sex. The same penalty was prescribed for both the man and the woman. Under that statute both a Negro man and a white woman were convicted. The man appealed on the ground that the statute infringed his constitutional rights to equal protection of the laws under the 14th Amendment.

Mr. Justice Field, in delivering the opinion of the Court, said:

"Equality of protection under the laws implies not only accessibility by each one, whatever his race, on the same terms with others to the courts of the country for the security of his person and property, but that in the administration of criminal justice he shall not be subjected, for the same offense, to any greater or different punishment. * * * Whatever discrimination is made in the punishment prescribed in these two sections is directed against the offense designated, and not against the person or any particular color or race. The punishment of each offending person whether white or black, is the same."

The statute, in the present case is not directed against the offense, but against one of the offending persons.

The Supreme Judicial Court of Massachusetts, in *Re Opinion of the Justices* (1911) 207 Mass. 601 said:

"The fact that a man is white or black, or yellow is not a just and constitutional ground for making certain conduct a crime in him, when it is treated as permissible and innocent in a person of a different color."

In Bolling vs. Sharpe, (1954) 347 U. S. 497, the Supreme Court of the United States stated that classifications based solely upon race must be scrutinized with particular care, since they are constitutionally suspect. It reaffirmed the principle

"that the Constitution of the United States, in its present form, forbids, so far as civil and political rights are concerned, discrimination by the General Government, or by the States, against any citizen because of his race. * * * "

It is argued on behalf of the State in this case that since marriage between the races is unlawful, under Art. 27 sec. 466, a child begotten by parents of different races must necessarily be illegitimate, and therefore the penalties of the bastardy laws apply to the man involved, thus equalizing the situation as between the sexes. The argument seems to this Court to be fallacious, for the bastardy statute applies to men and women of all races without discrimination. Furthermore, the bastardy statute prescribes no penalty at all upon either the putative father or the mother if bond be given to the State for the support of the child. Code, Art. 12, sec. 8, 10.

Although it is perfectly clear, as stated in argument, that no one has a constitutional right to beget or bear an illegitimate child, this case is not concerned with such a question, but with the question of discrimination by reason of imposing different penalties upon persons of different race or sex for the same conduct. See Plunkard vs. State (1887) 67 Md. 364.

This statute applies unequally to the conduct which it prohibits, in that it penalizes one class of guilty persons solely on the grounds of race. In the opinion of the Court the statute is unconstitutional and void, since it violates the principle of equal protection of the law under the 14th Amendment to the Constitution of the United States.

For the above reasons, the motion of the defendant to dismiss the indictment is granted.

Chapter Nine:
Epilogue

At last, almost four years after we met, the Billy's were together the way we were supposed to be – as a family. Shirley and I were finally happily married and had our baby with us. We were living at 523 North Chapel Street in East Baltimore in a 2-bedroom house – one for our son and one for us. I was ecstatic. I had a beautiful wife and a good-looking baby boy. We were living in an area that was much different from Bradford Street where I lived with my first wife. Our neighbors were even beginning to accept us living on the block. The woman who had called the police because I had white women in the house began talking to us. One neighbor babysat while Shirley and I went to work.

The house we lived in became the most popular house on the block, especially when the "Honey Boys" were there to rehearse. A singing group in those days was a real treat for people. The "Honey Boys" were looked up to because they were considered celebrities who had cut a record that was playing on the radio. We kept our front door open during practice and outside a crowd would gather to hear Calvin "Khaki" Kollette (lead), Roland "Big Boy" Jackson (bass), Dixon Stokes (baritone), and John "Prince" Billy (first tenor). The neighbors on Chapel Street didn't have to listen to the radio to hear the Honey Boys singing our hit songs "Never Lose Faith in Me" and "Bippity Bop." Even Shirley's brother and his wife came over on weekends and with our neighbors watched as the Honey Boys practiced. I'll never forget our house on Chapel Street.

About a year after we brought Johnny home, Shirley became pregnant again and our second child, another handsome boy, Gregory Gerald Billy, was born. All I wanted to complete our happy family was a baby girl. Soon, my wish came true and Terri Ann, our BEAUUUU-T-FUL daughter was born.

"The Honey Boys"
**(Recorded *Never Lose Faith in Me/Vippity Vop* on
Modern Records in 1955.)**
*Calvin "Khaki" Kollette (lead), Roland "Big Boy"
Jackson (bass), Dixon Stokes (baritone), and John
"Prince" Billy (first tenor).*

By this time, we knew we needed a bigger house. We decided that if we were going to move, we were going to buy, not rent, our next house. In 1960, we moved to 2107 Southern Avenue, in Morgan Park, where we live today. It was a wonderful, integrated neighborhood in which to raise our children. We were delighted because the schools were mixed. This is exactly what Shirley and I had always hoped for our children. We began to realize that with our determination and our togetherness, nothing was going to stop us from being successful.

Over the years, we really worked hard to get what we wanted but we always did it together. In 1973, we opened a grocery store at 2609 List Avenue. In 1974, we opened a record shop at 4608 Harford Road. For several years, Shirley managed the grocery store and I managed the record shop. After experiencing a couple of armed robberies at the grocery store, in 1982 we decided to sell it. We sold the record shop in 1984.

For almost 20 years, Shirley and her Mom did not correspond. They were estranged. When Shirley moved in with me on Chapel Street, her mother stopped speaking to her. She told her then, that she could come home at anytime, but she had to be by herself. One memorable moment in our early relationship that we both could never forget was when we were together on Chapel St. Her mother and stepfather knocked on the door. We did not answer. Shirley was afraid of what would happen if we did.

It was not until after we had the grocery store that Shirley and I had a long talk. I urged her to call her Mom and let her know that she was fine. I lost my mother when I was nine years old and I so much wanted Shirley to get back together with hers. I wanted Shirley to let her mother know that her daughter had not married a slouch. She also had to know that our marriage was a success. We loved each other then and we still do.

Shirley finally called her mother and arranged for us to come visit. After that visit, Shirley made weekly visits and did things to create a relationship, but her mother would always do or say something that hurt her. Once, after our children were born, and her brother had moved his family out of state, she commented to Shirley: "I'm so sorry your brother moved away because I miss the kids. After all, they're my only grandchildren." It was because of her bigotry that our children did not meet their grandmother until they were adults. She refused to see them.

Shirley's mother never hugged her, never kissed her. On her deathbed in 1988, she said: "Shirley, I love you!" Although these were words Shirley needed to hear, she describes how she felt when she heard them "My legs got weak and I almost fell to the ground." To me she said: " John, you've been better to me than my own son." These were words I was proud to hear.

In the year 2000, I retired after working 30 years as a truck driver for a local liquor distributing company. Shirley retired from her position of teller at Bank of America in 2001. They employed her for 18 years.

After many years, Shirley and I are pleased that a relationship has developed among us, our children, and my two oldest children from my first marriage.

Today, our children have given us seven grandchildren who are very much a major part of our lives. We never miss the chance to instill in them the lesson we tried to instill in our children – stand firm for love and for justice.

On June 21, 2008, Shirley and I will celebrate fifty years of marital bliss. Despite prejudice, racism, harassment, and hate from both white and black Americans that was an expected part of being in an interracial relationship, Shirley and I feel ours is truly a blessed marriage. Considering that we met in 1954, we often wonder what are the odds of our love lasting and us still being together, totally happy and completely committed to each other.

AIN'T LOVE GRAND???

Mr. and Mrs. John Moses Billy & Family
(Terri, Gregory, Johnny,)

The Billy's: June, 11, 2006
(Left to Right)
John, Terri, Shirley, (Behind Shirley) Gregory, Johnny

JOHN AND SHIRLEY BILLY
2006